Does A Dress Have A Life?

Millie Hiatt is a multi-faceted jewel, and each facet presents a unique and interesting revelation. Reflecting light from within as well as from without. Her strength, energy, and creativity are boundless. She is a poet, storyteller, actor, teacher, and mentor. Her work reflects an honest, loving, and unapologetic view of life, love, and family. She offers her work to friends for critique with the aim of making each piece stronger. She listens but never loses her own voice or intent. She mentors new writers by challenging them to polish and dig until they have achieved their best work. She speaks to her students honestly but without judgment-an approach that garners respect from those who work with her. Little did I know that when, just out of curiosity, I dropped into the very first Spoken Word event, a group Millie founded, that for the next ten years I would be collaborating, learning, and the grateful recipient of her friendship.

Friends, Family, and New Friends,

"Does a Dress Have a Life" is a collection of poems and short stories I wrote as therapy— a way to process the years of my life when I wanted to give up, crawl into a hole, and let life pass me by. Processing these poems and stories was like a treatment or a healing process. I hope this book will be of encouragement to you.

A fantastic director, Terri Ingalls, had a vision for my work. She saw it as a stage show. With hard work and a shit-ton of practice, this series became a one-act play. "Does a Dress Have a Life?" was originally performed on an outdoor stage at the Cherry Orchard Theater. What a healing performance it was for me and many audience members! I have performed this one-act play for two years now in many cities.

As you read, please notice the notes along the page edges. These special annotations are a testament to the collaborative nature of this work, mostly between my director and me. Some memos are "from me to me" to ensure I didn't stray from my dream. If you are striving to facilitate a healing journey for yourself, please don't give up. Survive and build your life— whether using dress slacks, a perky pantsuit, jeans, stilettos, flip-flops, or boots. Your survival can give them **life**.

xo xo xo

your Sister of the Wind

Millie Hiatt

1978

2024

An Honest Poem

Hi, my name is Millie.
I was named after my great-grandmother.
I tell strangers I meet to call me "Silly Millie"
because I want them to remember my name.
I love Christmas and parties, but not necessarily in that order.

I change my hair color often.
Blonde to be able to hide my intelligence like my mom did.
Brown to command a room like my grandmother did.
… and Red, much later in life, to show my dominance like my sister did.
I often chameleon my hair; it's standing on a pink plaid Christmas tree skirt, asking for a
vacation.

I survived the weight of white male privilege.
It scared me, but it never penetrated my soul.
The broken window pane that was my family,
carried me to a higher ground.

I took a nap there and then traveled higher, only to slide back down.
I treat my words like laughter, hoping they can fill someone else's sad spot with joy.
I am forever changing.
Sometimes for the worst, but sometimes for the best.

I love a house full of company.
I love a refrigerator full of food.
I love my family.
And for the first time in a long time, I love myself.

I have been single, married, divorced, and then married again.
I have been pregnant five times, and only one baby chose to grow beyond 9 months.

I have very big emotions.
I am deafening. I laugh aloud a lot.
My laughter is so big it leaks out of me like a faucet that has dripped so long, no one
bothers to fix it.

I turned 50 recently.
It didn't hurt my heart as much as I thought it would.
It did hurt my bones just like I thought it would.

When I wake up in the morning, I remind myself what day it is.
Keeping track is more of a tick than anyone knows.
I find myself seeking the company of Joy,
but Joy seems to be interested in another woman who is much prettier than I am.

Recently, Joy has shown some angsty teens that it is okay to be weird and also write.
And that they can trust me.
After all, **weird** is in.

I quote movies and songs all the time.
Occasionally, someone notices how I use that force.

Secretly, I want to be cool, very cool.
I am afraid I am not cool anymore.
My daughter is cool; I gave her the best of me, and I am not sure I have any cool left.

I am always happy twice a day. Sometimes more, but never less than two times.
First, when I wake up and realize I am still alive. That air is in my lungs, and my feet found
a space above ground to plant themselves,

And

Then again at night when I get to go back to bed. I get to write, read, and listen to words.
They somehow feed me.

My Grandparent's store in Chloe, West Virginia

DOES A DRESS
HAVE A
LIFE

Does a Dress Have a Life?

A gift from a *cousin* in Oregon. . .
The note read: I hope "Millie in Mayberry" loves it as much as I did.
I had created this persona during Covid—
to share clothes and tips and tricks across the internet with my family and friends.
While in lockdown, these daily internet discussions helped keep me going.
They kept me in touch with people that Covid prevented me from "touching."

The dress fit me perfectly.
I washed it and hung it in my closet, and it became a regular participant in my dress rotation.
The dress was then borrowed by a friend who needed it to cross the waterless sea.
The dress traveled from NC to VA and then all the way to California.

When it was returned, I washed it and hung it back in my closet as I had done before.
Before long, I pulled the dress out and slipped it over my body as I had done so-o-o many times before.
However, this time it felt different. Lighter. It sat just slightly above my skin, and it felt energized.

This dress. . .
this dress. . .
. . . now had a life of its own.

A Perfect Size 8

I'm a perfect size eight_
They always slide right on
high and tight
flat and frilly
and everything in between

It is unimportant the cost or the comfort_
The contour and feel are amazing
often comforting

If there is a new color
a new brand
a new style
I get excited_
a slingback
or peep toe

They all feel good when you're having a bad day_
or a bad week
or a bad year

Finding the right pair of shoes_
can sometimes be all you need
to change your perspective

Your moments or your moment's
moments_ arrange and rearrange it
and then you can stand on it

A good foundation sets the stage for the_
build
the rebuild
the reface
the reboot. . .

The NEW SHOE

Yeast Rolls

Everybody has a part of their body they like.
If you personally have not discovered what part of your body it is that you like.
Perhaps you should spend some time alone to discover it.

I mean, maybe you like the third toe on your left foot,
the way your hair parts perfectly over your right ear, or
the perfect shape your knuckles make when you ball up your fist.

They remind you of the day you punched your bully square in the
nose, near the Merry-Go-Round, in 6th grade.
Maybe you stood proud with pleasure as they cried outside tears,
instead of inside tears like you did.

I like my hands,
they look like my grandmothers,
the way they looked when I first came to live with her,
not the way they looked the day I got married or
the day she held my daughter for the 1st time and the last time,
but strong and full of energy.

I like my arms,
they are big and soft, and when I give hugs with them,
I try to imagine
I am wrapping a blanket around the person I am hugging and
I am squeezing all their troubles away.

Oh, and I like my butt,
 It's squishy, like a newly baked bread.
Not sourdough, but more like yeast rolls.
I hope people appreciate it the way I do.

Please find out what you absolutely love about yourself,
 I am sure someone else will love it,
 just as much as I love freshly baked yeast rolls.

By God

I was born in West Virginia, West, by God, Virginia.

I grew up in the most rural town, in the most rural community.
I grew up in the backwoods country.

And when you look at the stereotypical suit that I put on every day
you look at my hair, my nails, and my shoes

and you

assume,

assume. . .

I was born with a silver spoon, and I <u>was born</u> privileged.
Well, you see, I believe I was.

I was born out of an unwed union.
I was born to a teenage MOM.

I was born to "Know and to NO
what you can and can
NOT have."

I was born poor.
I was born in a struggle.

I was born to a mom who was addicted and afflicted
by a society-made demon.

I was born to "Know and to NO
what you can and can
NOT have."

My high school class had 100 kids.
All of them had the same skin color as me.
All of them were from the same side of the tracks as me.

You see,
I know the good side of the track.
I know the bad side of the track,
and
I also know the poison side of the track.

Once you have witnessed
the upside and the downside of life,
you are slower to judge by the facade you see,

and

more at what you know.

I was born to "Know and to NO
what you can and
can NOT have."

You feel differently about judgments,
and you think differently about privileges,
and you accept differences about your roots.

Do not judge me
by the leaves on my tree.

Do not judge me
by the roots of my trunk.

I was born to "Know and to NO

what you can and can

NOT have."

Judge me when you know me,

Look at as many
people in the
audience as you
can

NOT

When

You

See

Me!

My first Chicken!

Chicken Lot

Growing up in rural West Virginia, I had my fair share of feeding the cows, putting out scratch for the chickens, and slopping the hogs. I would drive the hay wagon through the fields while the neighbor boys would pick up square bales to feed all our animals through the winter. I told my grandmother that when I graduate from college, the only animal I want to feed is myself. I did not want to be on a farm anymore. So, the day I graduated from college, I loaded up my car and moved to the metropolis of Winston-Salem. I lived there for 5 years. And 5 years is all it took for me to miss West Virginia. I missed the hills, I missed the trees, I missed the animals, and I missed my family.

One day, my husband asked me, "What would make you feel better and less homesick? Do you miss the chickens? "

I answered with a definitive "Yes!"

He nodded and grinned, "Do you miss feeding them?"

I said, "NO!" Then I tried to explain. "I miss gathering the eggs. I want to be like the little girl on the cover of the Sears, Roebuck Catalog." This giant mail-order book came out several times a year, and you could order clothing, household items, and other stuff. This was before the internet took over catalog shopping. Around Easter, the catalog would arrive by mail, and there would be a little girl on the cover in a beautiful dress wearing white gloves and holding a basket of eggs.
"I want to be that little girl. I only want to gather the eggs."

He said, "I think I can fix that."

My husband built me a chicken mansion. Yes, that is right, a chicken mansion. He put in an automatic watering system. He put in an automatic feeder. The only thing I had to do was gather the eggs!

One evening, I came home from work, and my husband told me he was taking me out to dinner. He was taking me "out on the town." I told him that sounded great, I just must gather the eggs first."

He suggested I change my shoes before going to the chicken lot. I had on a dress and flip-flops. I cocked my head to the side and announced, "I will be fine."

He asked if I was sure, and I assured him it would be all right. After all, I was just going to get a few eggs. Then, I walked to the chicken lot and began putting eggs into my basket—1, 2, 3, 4, 5, 6, 7, 8. . .The rooster jumped upon my back as I reached for the last egg. I threw the egg basket into the air and hit the ground with a lone egg in my hand. Gathering my wits about me, I begrudgingly stood up. **I was covered in chicken shit,** and to make matters worse, my ankle was starting to swell and throb. I screamed for my husband, and he came running down the hill to see what was happening.

Cooly and calmly, he took one look at my ankle and said, "Well, that is going to need an x-ray."

Tears welled up in my eyes. I finally said, "Okay," and hobbled toward the truck.

I heard my husband's voice behind me, and he did not sound sympathetic. "Whoaah, you are not getting into my truck covered in chicken shit!" He then unhooked the automatic watering system and sprayed me off with the hose.

I do not know if you know anything about well water, but it is 60 degrees coming straight out of the ground. So, here I was, cold, soaking wet, crying with a throbbing ankle, and watching my husband look at me with an "I told you so grin!"

He said to me, "You know? What they say is true."

With a quivering lower lip, and a deep breath, I asked wearily, **"Wh-a-t**?"

"One egg in hand is better than eight broken eggs in a basket."

Then with a big grin, he picked me up and sat me in his truck. "Ready for our night on the town?"

get coat & go to table
for next poem

Time Is Relevant

Considering this thing, we
call Time and an Eternity—

Skunk spray
A baby's first word
A paper cut
The first flower of spring
A belly laugh
A tear on 9-11

It's been an eternity since
I was standing on a kitchen chair, learning to make biscuits.
Time lasted longer then.
It tasted better, also.

Getting to 16 took forever.
You were chasing me, trying to wipe tobacco juice on my dress.
My. . .prom. . .dress.

I ran like a 6-year-old
who stole the remote control on Saturday morning.

When college caught my eye
a four-year degree felt like a vanishing dream that
somehow,
surprisingly,
came true.

The day you were diagnosed taught me how short 53 years
were. They said 6 months. You took 2 years.
She was determined to see my baby girl walk.

You were always stubborn like that
when looking at time and trying to define it in
years, days, hours, and minutes.
It's completely relative to what you are doing,
how you are feeling, and
what you are experiencing.

Stay true and take as much time as you need.

Time

Is

Relevant!

My Grandmother

My Love

Did you know that my love comes from a strange place?

I love those who love me
I love those who use me

My love comes from a strange place.

I love those who hurt me
I love those who are hurting
I love those who don't know how to love me

My love comes from a strange place.

I love you

and

I love you

and

I love myself

My love comes from a strange place.

A place of growth
A place of pain
A place that often leaves my cup half-
empty and a little worn with wear.

I will love you, strange or not.

That One Boy

I was the only boy my grandfather took time to love.
He taught me to fish, hunt, and work on cars.

This made me more of a boy's friend than a girlfriend.

The boys always liked me
because I didn't complicate things.

Maybe that's why this boy
Liked me. . .

He lived close enough to me that we knew each other,
but far enough away, we never belonged to each other.

He was easy, like the 5th shot of whisky and
hard like your first-time whiff of whisky.

We were "real" with one another.
*Yes-s, that is the exact spot; don't you **dare** stop.*

Our hookups were epic.

Sophomore year
very short skirt
earth science
back corner table
9:45 on a Wednesday morning.

He finished the school day by casually putting his fingers in his mouth or
running them under his nose every time I saw him.

We spoke in code in front of all our friends.
He would say something like…

I heard you are grounded 'till November?
What did you do this time?

Which translates:
Meet me at 11 pm and tell me what you
want *to do?*
I would then have to quickly think up some clever response to answer
that translated only to him.

I would say something like:
I wrecked my bike trying to drown the neighbor's cat behind the barn again.

Everyone standing around would erupt in laughter; we were known for our comedic
banter.

None of them ever knew about us.
We were *friends with benefits* before it was a movie, a trend, or a hashtag.

I wasn't like my classmates.

I didn't want to settle down,

marry a boy, and pop out a few smelly brats.

I didn't even want a dog.

I wanted to be free.

I want to swallow and taste life.

I wanted to experience and enjoy the fruits of the world
… on my own terms.

Calhoun County High School Grantsville, West Virginia

Ruby Slipper Fringe Festival

February 20th, 2016

My Crazy Mama

Ok, a show of hands---- how many people here have a crazy mama?

walk toward crowd

    not 'a show your new boyfriend photos of you on the potty chair-crazy
    not 'a sit 6 rows behind you in the movies on your first date-crazy
    not even 'a walk up on the school bus and confront a bully-crazy
    but 'a lock and unlock all the windows and doors 17 times to be sure you're safe-crazy
    make and remake the bed 7 times to be sure it's perfect-crazy
    let's hide under the bed when someone knocks on the door because it is dark outside
    crazy

17 & 7 were my mama's numbers.
I don't know why 17.
But number 7? That was the magic one;
7 meant completion.
Nothing was complete in just one try.   *— deep breath —*

    you see, i have lived my life in strange halves—
    the half i spent with my Mom — birth to about 10 years,
    the half i spent with my grandmother— 10 years 'till about 20
    the half i spent with my 1st husband . . . hmm .... let's skip him, okay?.

Let me tell you about good-crazy

    Happy second marriage, 2 grown kids, three grandbabies,
    a middle-aged and menopausal lady—now that JUST might be the NEW crazy.
    I can't wait to see what the next half has in store for me.
    I mean, does anyone KNOW anything about HOT FLASHES??

Please understand— with me—--the 1st half-life was with my crazy teenage Mom—
Well, she **was** my Mom. I didn't know she was crazy, 'till way later in life.
I just knew she was my best friend, and I didn't understand why
social services wanted to take her away from me. . .

not me away from her, but her away from me
not me away from her, but her away from me
not me away from her, but her away from me

Then I assumed every mom smoked weed and used a bit of the white powder to fix their
nerves.
I thought all families had wild parties every weekend, and when the police showed up, we
knew the party was over.
It wasn't until I started public school that I discovered just how crazy she was.

The first time I remember IT was in second grade.
Mrs. Franetic said I wasn't in any trouble, but the brownies with "herbs"
were inappropriate for school, and I could not hand out during the party what my Mama
made.
My teacher said it would be best if I passed out her cookies instead.

That was the first time social services visited my house.

The social worker asked me if I was scared and I said, "No."
Because I knew Mama always locked the doors 17 times.

The social worker asked if I was hungry. I said, "No."
Because Mama always ran the microwave.
When she was *coming down*, my house was *munchies central*.

The social worker asked me if I thought. . . maybe,
just maybe,
my MAMA was

SICK.
SICK.
SICK.

i said, "No." I knew how much medicine she took to stay well.
i knew the efforts she put in 7 times & 7 ways for things to be complete.
i knew how much medicine she needed to wake up and how much medicine she
needed to pass out

After all, mama needed me.
                    She needed me
                    She needed me.

She needed me to help weigh the "dime bags" to correct them.
Because I was the one who was good in math.
She needed me to tell her when she wasn't safe to drive.
Because sometimes it wasn't.

She needed me.

She needed me to recheck the car 7 times to be sure the engine wasn't running.
Because she trusted me when I said, "MAMA, it's fine!"

She believed me-
She believed me-
She believed *in* me-

She needed me to be her aspiration.
She needed me. . . When they took her from me, I was about 10 years old, and mostly so
was she. . .

I was told that my Mama was in pain and needed help, but I was the one hurting—
hurting—hurting.

Truly, by today's standards, she had a disease:

  a bipolar disease
  a social disease
  an economic disease
  Asperger's
  ADHD & ADD
  a lack of proper education disease
  a free will, hippy, gypsy disease
  a mixed up and messed up disease
  a disease that was never diagnosed or treated with modern medicine.

She self-medicated, witch-doctored, and drank her demons away.
She died 3 months before her 54th birthday.

Over the years, she sporadically came in and out of my life.
Mama was the loudest, most distinct voice at a dinner party.

She was drunk during my high school graduation but once saved my best friend's life.
She was high at my first wedding, but she cried with me when my grandmother died
because we didn't know who would hold our family together.

She snuck "weed" in my daughter's teething ring because she was sure it would help.
She told my first boyfriend if you hold a butterfly too tight, it will surely die and never fly.
I think that may have been the pills talking.

Once, she also told me I was the only positive thing to ever come out of between her legs.
I believed her.

Yes! She was crazy.

She really was.

She was

MY MAMA

Kent State

She was born into a middle-class working family.

My mother was the child of a man who was retired military,
a prison security guard, and a
leather-saddle-making-man.

She was the child of a woman who was Baptist- raised,
A college graduate, well-educated, a teacher, and homemaker.

She grew up 11 miles from Kent State, and she was 14 when the massacre took place.

She was watching with the observers.
She had cut school
One of the many cut-school days.

When it happened, she ran, tears stinging her eyes to the beaten-up Chevy van she had
hitched a ride in.
She sat on the floor squeezing the shag carpet between her finders, rocking back and
forth, screaming why, why, why?

She couldn't tell anyone about that day; she wasn't supposed to be there.
She was with some much older boys, and everyone had been drinking.

As my grandmother held my mom, and swayed in the dark night, she said,
"No more TV for you, young lady. The news is much too graphic.

Kent State

May 4th of 1970
On this day, we fired upon ourselves
67 shots were fired

Killing 4 students:

Jeffery
Allison
William
&
Sandra

Wounding nine

My mother was protesting war and
begging for peace.

I am not sure my mother ever recovered from that day.
When I was a child, she trusted me with that day's story many times.

With her careful storytelling, I could feel the dept of her worry and fear.
I could hear the trembles in her voice.
The soft beads of sweat upon her upper lip told of the panic.
I could smell blood and feel her pain.

How will my children know their struggles?
As mothers, we do not want to see our children suffer pain, have their bellies ache from
hunger, do without shelter, or feel unsafe in their own skin. We know that pain.

With pain comes understanding, and with experience, comes compassion, which breeds
growth. And growth, real growth, means change.

Grow Seeds / Produce Twigs / Put forth Buds and with the new growth will beg for
change.
Make branches that withstand the winter snow.

Make trees that bear our spring fruit.

Tho' sometimes,
Seeds may blow away, buds may die,
twigs bend and crack,
branches can break, and once in a while, a tree can die, but does it? Really? Is a tree in
the dead of winter dead or only dormant?

Grow ideas for change in the presence of a great support.

Understand the way it stands.

Know it has stood.
Kent State is still standing.
My mother is gone,
Her pain grows inside of me.

And

    I

        still

           stand.

My mother's senior photo

My Mother's Skin

I am not her, and she is not me.
Her skin could not be mine, and mine could be no part of her.
Her skin was used up,
      thickened and thinned,
      even bare in some places.
She frantically searched for cotton.
Cotton soft enough to cover the
      empty spaces between the intentions of her skin, and its actuality.
Fixated on pain and finding highs too high to get down from.

I have no tracks on my skin,
      only the tracks I have crossed that follow me.
I have no bruises across my skin,
      except the ones that were her fault. and I had obviously asked for.
I have no visible black and blue in my pigment,
      only rose-colored tears that escape but do not fall out.

They are never allowed to hit the page,
      for my sword has written them away.
Perhaps the tissue that binds our skin is ambiguous to us,
      the more we repel it and the tighter it bonds itself to us.
Take it with both hands,

      twist it into change and use it to fertilize your grace.

When I put my skin on, sometimes her skin shows through.
      No matter how thick I build up my base, she still seeps through.
Alas, I aspire to embrace her love, and her need to survive
      love without conditions, and secure her space above the high.

I find myself high in the magic that hides between the words.

My daughter's senior photo

My Daughter's Skin

I wish her skin to be strong— no fierce!
And for her skin to be thick, thicker than mine.

We always want more for our offspring, to have more, and to be more.
But is it better?
I think maybe— Yes?
or
I guess maybe— No?

If you are too hard, you can't let anyone in or allow anyone through.
Your experiences, your relationships and your skins will mold and shape you.
My daughter says I care too much and give too much of myself to strangers.
She says I gave this to her like it's the flu or uncontrolled infection.

One without a vaccine.
You know. . . vaccines. They give us relief from a disease but only to provide us with side
effects from a different disease.
Her skin is progressing beautifully, her baby skin is shedding, and her adult skin is
growing.
She is picking and tearing at it daily. I take a deep breath and refuse to step in and stifle
her.
She grows new skin daily.
I see all the people in her life peeking through her skin.

They look like passport stamps, depicting her journey and showing her paths.

She often wants to change her skin.
She always wants more.
I remember that age, growing so fast you tear.
Matching your friends and then becoming an individual.
I can't wait for her to learn the art of multiple skins.

My senior photo

My Skin

I put on my skin for work, I stretch it over my depression,
like a mail-order bride.

I place my freedom-washed feet inside the corporate skin.
I cover my tattoos, my piercings, and my thoughts.
And I march from 8 AM to 5 PM.
Tick tock, tick tock,
I work the clock.

When evening comes, and freedom finds me, I rip the skin off that binds me.
I set my heart free, and I show me. But do I really?

I put on the skin of **wife.**
I put on the skin of **mother.**
I put on the skin of **daughter.**
I put on the skin of **faithful servant.**

Would you like a drink? May I fill up your cup?
Are you hungry? Are you comfortable? Would you like a pillow?

Being a female born to be raised by my maternal grandmother,
A survivor of the depression.
The skin that is stretched around us is for servitude to others.

But is that who the real me is?
Do I lie when I pull each skin over me? Do I lie when I pull those skins off?
Do I lie when I lay down and lose a layer of skin?
I ask you. Can you see through the skins to help me find the skin I want to live in?

A Half Sister, An Ex--step Sister, and Several Sisters of the Wind

When I see you with some of God's creations,   *arms wide open*
I truly see a talent to love unconditionally.

To correct so softly that they may grow uninhibited.
To pray a prayer of love and tenderness
 despite any physical or emotional differences.   *point*

To be so sensitive to the spirit, God must be conspiring with you daily.

My soul seeks nourishment of a raw and natural type.
 A type that you can't hide in a bush,
under a barrel, or even on a church pew.

Your giving waters of words bathe all around you in confidence and radiance.

You walk in the light so brightly that no one sees the slightly open closet door where you hang your insecurities.

Friends,
acquaintances,
and family,
sometimes they never see your heart.

You can easily hide your true nature from almost anyone.
But a soul sister doesn't need all that fluff.
I will love you when you don't love yourself.

Thank you for seeing the broken sister in me.

I am forever

your sister of the wind

See Yourself

Be a Dinosaur, they said
Your skirt is too
Beautiful for your closet.

Your pants are
made for dancing.

Don't show so much
personality.

Make them work
for the inner you.

fist

Cover up.
Leave something
under your bed to feed the jealousy that stands
in the mirror next to you.

look over sholder

Don't eat too
MUCH cardboard;
it will stop up all the works—
leaving you flat and dull.

Drink lots of
sunshine.
Plait that shit in your braids.

Men like women with some
intelligence
in their bones.
They carry the weight of their confidence in it.

finish hands on hips

Mindmares

Talking to my friends about my childhood sometimes gets hard.
When talking to a stranger, I simply say my grandparents raised me.
When talking to an acquaintance, I often say my childhood was difficult.
Closer friends get more. Bit by bit. Piece by piece. Story by story. I open-up.

Sometimes I say I was assaulted.
Sometimes I say my mother just wasn't ready to raise a child.
Sometimes I say I am a survivor.
Sometimes I clearly refuse to say what exactly.

I am a survivor of . . . only that I survived.

I always feel the story would be more interesting if I had
                survived being trapped in a dungeon by a Toothless Troll,
                narrowly escaping with my life at dawn as he went back under his bridge.

When a more accurate reflection of the truth would be that
I narrowly escape my *mindmares* by crawling under a porch.

Mindmares are what I have always called them because I am rarely asleep.

My mindmares

Mindmares are these thoughts that everyone knows what happened to me,
and they can see the movies of my life being projected above my head.

I know I am the person I am today because of the things I have experienced.

                Good and Bad
                      or
                Good and Evil,
          however, you want to name your demons.

The first few years after…

The event
The attack
The betrayal
The incident. . .

I don't think I was surviving. I was merely existing.

Lately I want to chant, yell, and scream.
I want to tell people.
I want to show people that you can be different,
you can be— ok, you can survive.

But to make the words come out of my mouth, to utter the words . . . still today,
 I find them difficult even when speaking with very dear friends
        that I adore …
        Ones I trust…
        Ones I know love me and care about my wellbeing
        and my ability to fight off trolls.

But mindmares. . .

I still often sidestep the issue, and I sidestep the questions.

In the early 80s you didn't talk about family issues: you didn't discuss your feelings.

A very upstanding attorney in rural West Virginia told me to stop crying. . .
"It happened, it's over, now go on living in spite of them."
 I spent two nights in the hospital because the one person on the planet who was
        supposed to protect me— didn't.
And mostly that person was not capable of doing so.

I screamed for help.
I fought.
I fought, really hard.

I could see my mother passed out just outside my bedroom door on the floor.

One too many lines of coke mixed with one too many
        bottles of Jack had forced her into a deep sleep.
After the last time he hit me, he slid off my bloody body, and he began throwing up.

I crawled across my bedroom floor to the doorway into the bathroom.
I then found a way to stand.
I walked down the hallway, and by the time my hand hit the screen door, I was running.
I heard the familiar bang of the old screen door as it banged closed behind me.

I ran to the neighbor's house and crawled under their porch steps.
I remember thinking, *I will hide here till morning.*
It would be very impolite to wake them in the dead of the night.

I forgot about their dog...
I remember lots of barking and this 'ol dog licking the blood,
        Sweat, and tears from my face, hands, and legs.

Was I angry about what happened? YES!
Did I ever get over being mad, angry? Yes.
Did I find a way to forgive my mom? Also, yes.

My name is Millie and I am a rape survivor.
I promise that. . .
Mindmares
        can
            someday
                go
                    away.

Regroup
Get some water
Survive!

The Decision in Three Parts

PART 1

Hey there, can you tell us
Your name?

What is it that brought everyone here today?
I see.

How long has your mother been sundowning?
Oh, she doesn't have dementia, just some confusion.
 I understand.

Would you agree with me that being home alone is not safe?
I understand you must work, if there is anything, we all have debts.
Our loved ones are usually the hardest on the one they love the most.
So, where were you when she fell down the basement stairs?

PART 2

I am the best person to take care of her.
I don't want her to leave her home, our home.

I can't just quit my job.
I know she can't be home alone.

There is nothing wrong with her, she just gets a bit confused sometimes.
It's because she is just so angry with me; it will get better when she gets over her mad spell.

Um, I was unloading my groceries.

take off jacket —get
purse &
look for something that
isn't
there

PART 3

I am Willow. I live at 223 Maple Wood Drive. My phone number is 336-555-1212.

I am not allowed to get out of my chair without permission.

The baby was crying in the basement, and I figured the locks out, so I could open the basement door.

She is the one who locked me outta there, anyways it's **my** house.

These babies need me.

I can rock 'em better than anyone else. Lots better than her.

I am thirsty.

Could you get me another blanket?

I am cold.

Everything is so. . . cold.

A Mother's Mom

I always wanted to be a mother,
not a mother like my mother,
but a mother like my grandmother.

I always wanted to be a grandmother,
exactly like my grandmother, only slightly cooler.
I always admired her ability to love my mother
no matter what my mother did.
Her ability to love me no matter what I did.

She was a force of nature.
Fierce in her fire and calm in her correction.
She tried to control everything, even when she had no
control. She gently pushed in the direction she felt needed.

I began my journey to motherhood
with lots of ideas about what type of mother I would be.
I even had dreams about what type of grandmother I would
be. What I didn't consider was *what type of child I would get!*

Self-Worth

My own self-worth,
My own self-confidence.
I have them taped up and marked fragile.

They are inside my head
Safe and sound, slow dancing
to the tune of my grandmother's prayers.

"Rest easy baby, let God hold you,
He is all you need, breath slo-o-w,
He is here with us. . . "

Boxes are heavy, weighted with the comments I received
in passing . . .
Meaningless to the speaker, BUT a bludgeoned trauma to me
That is now inside my head.
So, I must smile a slo-o-w chuckle
The hate, the jealousy, the fear is nestled around my self-worth holding it hostage.

Perhaps live animal stickers should be placed on the boxes
Because doubt is a demon.
Living, breathing, walking around in a dress that is not black and is way too short,
You know you are not going to wear it out of the house anyway, kind of demon.
Leaving food on your plate because you don't want to be judged, kind of demon.

Pretending to be satisfied,
Holding a torch,
Crying inside,
Missing the dance,

Don't talk too loudly,
Take small pieces-
Only be seen kind of demon.

I am putting the boxes inside the tone of my grandmother's prayers,
I plan to float them above me.
Float them on the words of her prayers,
So, they can be lifted to God's ears far away from my head.

"Rest easy baby, let God hold you.
He is all you need, breath

S

     L

        O

          W

He is here with us."

BARBIZON School of Modeling—- a FINISHING SCHOOL

My grandmother raised me for the most part, and as I became a teenager, she began
looking for a finishing school. The problem was that it was the 1980s, and there were no
finishing schools. But my grandmother was determined that I would learn how to be a
lady.

She felt I needed to be " finished." I was different from my grandmother. Whereas she
was slim, alluring, and beautiful, I was. . . well, I was. . . fun. She sat at the kitchen table,
poring over the Charleston Gazette Newspaper with strong black coffee cooling and a
Virginia Slim freshly lit, waiting for her next drag. She read an ad in the paper from the
Barbizon School of Modeling.

The school's ad read:
Let Barbizon School of Modeling Make You a Lady!
We will teach you poise, purposeful standing,
and how to sit and walk gracefully. We will
teach you how to present yourself as a lady.

She took a nice long drag off her cigarette and said, "This, my dear, is what we need!"
She then took another puff of her half-burnt cigarette, looked at me intently and said,
"Listen. I married for love, baby. You? You should marry for money! But first, you must
learn to be a lady. No more *tom-boying*." So, then and there, my grandmother decided I
would attend the Barbizon School of Modeling. And I decided, like it or not, I **Would**
become whatever my grandmother wanted— with a smile!

She drove us forty-five minutes from our home in the country into Charleston, West
Virginia. She took me there to parade me in front of the Barbizon School instructors. The
Matron of the school was a very tall and wafer-thin lady who was smoking Virginia Slims
inside. . . the building. As she and my grandmother smoked and talked. The Matron said,
"She is not what we are looking for in a model. I am very sorry. "

In the age of Christie Brinkley and Janice Dickerson (grossly skinny models), I was not the
model type. Besides, I didn't want to be a model, and I did not want to "be finished." I
wanted to be Mary Lou Retton. A short and stocky gymnast from Fairmont, West Virginia,
who had just scored a perfect 10 in the 1984 Olympics. That is what I wanted to be . . . an

Olympic medal gymnast! Grandmother took a long and frustrated drag off her cigarette and asked the Matron of the school, "But can you finish her and make her into a lady?"

The Matron said, "Of course."

The Matron of the school explained to my grandmother that I didn't qualify for scholarships. Plus, unlike many students, I was not qualified to work for my tuition in print pictures and day modeling. But Grandmother was a fierce member of nature and could not be deterred. She would pay for me to attend the fancy school. Period.

She would often stand in the doorways smoking when I was in class over the next few years. She told the instructors, pointing at me, "Make sure this one gets it; I am paying for her to be here."

The other girls had "Look Books." These little books were filled with photos they had sold as a working model to pay for their tuition. My book didn't have any photos in it. My book was empty. So, Grandmother decided that every time we went shopping for clothes for the Barbizon School of Modeling, we would remove the tags from the dresses and glue them down in the book. They would be tags with very thin girls wearing the dresses in weird poses. I then had to practice emulating each pose for my grandmother and the instructors at the school to prove I was being finished.

Every so often, a department store shoot would be set up during our class times. It would be Kmart, Hills, Hecks, or LA Joes, usually coming to set up a t-shirt and underwear shoot. The Matron of the school knew they would not pick me, as well as Grandmother would not be pleased with me modeling t-shirts and underwear! Therefore, the Matron had a trunk of clothes for me to put on. They covered me from my neck to my ankles. I would pose and pose and pose, but no one took any actual photos.

I went to the Barbizon School of Modeling not one, not two, but three years. Each year, at the end of the term for our final exam, there would be a special garment project for the end-of-season runway/ catwalk. In the first year, my grandmother and I made a tea gown. Church socials were practiced in lieu of an actual tea party. We made a lovely floor-length satin gown for my winter school formal in year two. This event served as my "Introduction to Society." In my third year, my grandmother had something special in mind. She took me to a thrift store, and we picked out a very simple and reasonably priced wedding

gown. We then added beads, buttons, and lace all over it. She was finishing me!
Grandmother was preparing me for the future.

I never became a model. The Barbizon School of Modeling never published a photo of
me. Unlike high school, I never received a school letter jacket or class ring. I was never
featured on the cover of a magazine or catalog. Still between Grandmother and the
Barbizon School of Modeling I did learn poise, how to sit and walk gracefully, and most
importantly, confidence—how to be confident in my own skin.
AND . . .

how
    to
        make
          a
            dress
              have
                a
                  life . . .

Spoken Word promotes the preservation of oral presentation through poetry and storytelling. It encourages, supports, and aims to make all events actively non-competitive, non-judgmental, pro-diversity, anti-racist, LGBTQIA+ ally, and a fun, nurturing environment for writers of all levels!

To learn more about our group and other events scan the QR code below.